Promises
for
Grand-
parents

GW00320207

Harold Shaw Publishers
Wheaton, Illinois

"I will be your God
through all your lifetime,
yes, even when your hair is white with age.
I made you and I will care for you.
I will carry you along and be your Savior."
Isaiah 46:4, TLB

Introduction

In the Scriptures, old age is considered a blessing—a gift from God. As you grow older, it is a strong comfort to know that God never changes. He loves you with an everlasting love! The Scriptures are full of answers to the questions older people are asking today.

"How can I know God is still in control?"

"Am I of value to God?"

"How can I continue to have a significant ministry to other people?"

"Will God supply my financial needs?"

"How can I build a godly heritage for my children and grandchildren?"

"How can I be sure of eternal life?"

Promises for Grandparents is designed to help you find God's answers to these questions. As you use this book, these promises will become an integral part of your life, giving you comfort, hope, and joy.

As you open this book, ask yourself, "What is a specific concern in my life today?" Look through the list of questions in the Contents and find the one that echoes your concern. Then turn to the section that asks your question and read the selected Scriptures.

You may want to choose one verse which speaks specifically to your need. Copy it on a card, or perhaps even memorize it. Use the prayer pages at the back of the book to personalize the verse and to thank God for his promise to you.

The God who made you will continue to care for you all the days of your life. And this is just the beginning! Not even death can separate you from the love of God (Romans 8:38-39). An eternity of joy is waiting for you in heaven.

Contents

Who God Is to Me

When life seems overwhelming and it looks as if God isn't keeping his promises, how can I feel assured of his faithfulness? *24*

Sometimes it's hard to feel that God is listening when I pray. How can I know that God hears my prayers? *25*

It frustrates me to see bad things happen to good people. How can I be sure that God is fair? *26*

Who I Am to God

Sometimes I don't feel good about myself. Am I of value to God? *28*

How can I show God my love and respect? *29*

Sometimes I feel self-conscious because age has changed my appearance. How does God see me? *30*

I can't do all the things I did when I was young. What can I do for God now? *31*

I'm afraid that if someday I can no longer control my actions and speech, I might dishonor the Lord. *32*

When I'm feeling forgotten or unimportant, how can I feel encouraged that God hasn't forgotten me? *33*

Children and Grandchildren

My family has been important to me all my life. Does God value my children and grandchildren? *35*

How can my actions build a godly heritage for my children and their children? *36*

I worry about my children and my grandchildren. What can I do now to keep them growing in the Lord even after I'm not with them anymore? *37*

Sometimes I feel sad that I won't be able to look after my children and grandchildren for many more years. How can I feel assured that God will take care of them? *39*

At times I'm concerned about the tensions in some of my family relationships. How does God want me to respond? *41*

Although I have brought up my children to live godly lives, some of them are not living for God. How can I keep hoping for them? *42*

Some of the choices I made as a parent were damaging to my children. I know God has forgiven me, but can God turn my mistakes into something good for my children and their children? *44*

Although my children have families of their own, I want our extended family to grow together. How can we be unified? *45*

When I'm Hurting Physically

I feel alone with my physical pain; no one else can feel it with me. How can I know God is with me when I'm hurting? *48*

If I become inarticulate or confused, will I still be able to communicate with God? *49*

When I see those dear to me suffering, I sometimes doubt God's goodness. How can I be reminded that he is a caring God? *50*

Sometimes my ongoing physical discomfort makes me depressed or discouraged. How can I tap into the Source of joy when I feel down? *52*

Will God give me the strength to endure my sickness and pain? *53*

Sometimes, when I'm afraid or anxious, I feel physically ill. How can I feel secure and unafraid? *54*

When physical limitations prevent me from leaving the house, I stay at home and pray. How can I know my prayers will accomplish anything? *56*

Can the Lord help me rest at night when I am unable to sleep? *57*

On days when I feel physically weak, how can I help my faith grow strong? *58*

Sometimes I'm afraid that my physical limitations will be embarrassing to my loved ones. *59*

When Circumstances around Me Are Hard

As my life changes, I sometimes feel confused and unstable. Can God provide the guidance and safety I need? *61*

I feel anxious because others are making decisions for me. *63*

How can I find peace when I feel anxious about the unknown, uncertain things in life? *64*

As old friends and family members pass away or move away from me, I am often sad. How can I feel encouraged by God? *65*

Sometimes I worry about finances. Will God provide for my needs? *66*

It's hard for me not to worry about being a financial burden to my family. How does God want me to handle dependency? *67*

Sometimes I feel resentful when I see others enjoying comfort and wealth. Can God help me to be glad for them and thankful for what I have? *68*

How can I develop a deep and lasting faith—one that doesn't shift from day to day? *69*

Death and the Hope of Heaven

When I think about death, it seems so final. How can I know that I have eternal life? *71*

Even though I know I'll go to be with the Lord, sometimes I am afraid of dying. Can God relieve my fears about death? *73*

When I think about dying, I feel lonely. Will God be with me when I die? *74*

I'm looking forward to heaven. What will it be like? *76*

Many of my dearest friends and family members have died. Where can I find comfort? *77*

The Abundant Life

Most of my life is behind me now. Does God want me to make certain plans for the years ahead? *79*

I have received so much from God. What can I do for him? *81*

I haven't read the Bible much during my life. I have more time now. Will God really speak to me? *82*

For many, old age is a time of sadness and discomfort. How can I be full of joy? *84*

I seem to be spending more and more time alone. How can I turn this into something good rather than letting it get me down?   *85*

As I am becoming more limited in my ability to get out or to travel, how can I keep sharing my faith and my Christian experience with others?   *86*

Because of physical limitations, I am unable to serve the Lord in the way I used to. How can I serve him now? *88*

Now that I am older, I still want to get excited about life and be involved, but what do I have to look forward to? *90*

Who God Is to Me

God seems so awesome and powerful. How can I know God as my personal friend and Father?

"You will seek me and find me when you seek me with all your heart. I will be found by you, " declares the LORD. *Jeremiah 29:13-14, NIV*

To all who received him, who believed on his name, he gave power to become children of God. *John 1:12, RSV*

O Lord my God, many and many a time you have done great miracles for us, and we are ever in your thoughts. *Psalm 40:5, TLB*

The Spirit himself testifies with our spirit that we are God's children. *Romans 8:16, NIV*

As a father has compassion on his children, so the LORD has compassion on those who fear him; for he knows how we are formed, he remembers that we are dust. *Psalm 103:13-14, NIV*

When I have problems or my circumstances change, how can I know that God is still in control?

Even to your old age and gray hairs I am he, I am he who will sustain you. I have made you and I will carry you; I will sustain you and I will rescue you. *Isaiah 46:4, NIV*

Jesus Christ the same yesterday, and to day, and for ever. *Hebrews 13:8*

The LORD your God is he that goeth with you, to fight for you against your enemies, to save you. *Deuteronomy 20:4, KJV*

This plan of mine is not what you would work out; neither are my thoughts the same as yours! For just as the heavens are higher than the earth, so are my ways higher than yours, and my thoughts than yours. *Isaiah 55:8-9, TLB*

The Lord is still in his holy temple; he still rules from heaven. He closely watches everything that happens here on earth. *Psalm 11:4, TLB*

I am the LORD, I change not. *Malachi 3:6, KJV*

I want my faith to grow! How can I learn to trust in God?

Ah Lord GOD! behold, thou hast made the heaven and the earth by thy great power and stretched out arm, and there is nothing too hard for thee . . . Behold, I am the LORD, the God of all flesh: is there any thing too hard for me? *Jeremiah 32:17, 27, KJV*

Yours, O LORD, is the greatness and the power and the glory and the majesty and the splendor, for everything in heaven and earth is yours. Yours, O LORD, is the kingdom; you are exalted as head over all. Wealth and honor come from you; you are the ruler of all things. In your hands are strength and power to exalt and give strength to all. *1 Chronicles 29:11-12, NIV*

Every good and perfect gift is from above, coming down from the Father of the heavenly lights, who does not change like shifting shadows. *James 1:17, NIV*

Before you created the hills or brought the world into being, you were eternally God, and will be God forever. *Psalm 90:2, TEV*

When I go through dry periods in my spiritual life or times of struggle, how can I know God still loves me?

I have loved thee with an everlasting love: therefore with lovingkindness have I drawn thee. *Jeremiah 31:3, KJV*

God demonstrates his own love for us in this: While we were still sinners, Christ died for us. *Romans 5:8, NIV*

As the Father has loved me, so have I loved you. Now remain in my love. *John 15:9, NIV*

The LORD is merciful and loving, slow to become angry and full of constant love. *Psalm 103:8, TEV*

You are precious to me and honored, and I love you. *Isaiah 43:4, TLB*

Know therefore that the LORD your God is God; he is the faithful God, keeping his covenant of love to a thousand generations of those who love him and keep his commands. *Deuteronomy 7:9, NIV*

This is how God showed his love among us: He sent his one and only Son in the world that we might live through him. This is love: not that we loved God, but that he loved us and sent his Son as an atoning sacrifice for our sins. *1 John 4:9-10, NIV*

Sometimes when I sin, it's hard for me to believe that God will forgive me. How can I be sure that my sins aren't too many or too terrible to be forgiven?

If we confess our sins, he is faithful and just to forgive us our sins, and to cleanse us from all unrighteousness. *1 John 1:9, KJV*

O Lord, you are so good and kind, so ready to forgive; so full of mercy for all who ask your aid. *Psalm 86:5, TLB*

You are a forgiving God, gracious and compassionate, slow to anger and abounding in love. *Nehemiah 9:17, NIV*

Repent, then, and turn to God, so that your sins may be wiped out, that times of refreshing may come from the Lord. *Acts 3:19, NIV*

Listen! In this man Jesus, there is forgiveness for your sins! Everyone who trusts in him is freed from all guilt and declared righteous. *Acts 13:38-39, TLB*

Let the wicked forsake his way, and the unrighteous man his thoughts: and let him return unto the LORD, and he will have mercy upon him; and to our God, for he will abundantly pardon. *Isaiah 55:7, KJV*

As far as the east is from the west, so far has he removed our transgressions from us. *Psalm 103:12, NASB*

When life seems overwhelming and it looks as if God isn't keeping his promises, how can I feel assured of his faithfulness?

His divine power has given us everything we need for life and godliness through our knowledge of him who called us by his own glory and goodness. Through these he has given us his very great and precious promises, so that through them you may participate in the divine nature and escape the corruption in the world caused by evil desires. *2 Peter 1:3-4, NIV*

Let us hold firmly to the hope we profess, because we can trust God to keep his promise. *Hebrews 10:23, TEV*

No matter how many promises God has made, they are "Yes" in Christ. *2 Corinthians 1:20, NIV*

The God who made both earth and heaven, the seas and everything in them. He is the God who keeps every promise. *Psalm 146:6, TLB*

Sometimes it's hard to feel that God is listening when I pray. How can I know that God hears my prayers?

The righteous cry, and the LORD heareth, and delivereth them out of all their troubles. *Psalm 34:17, KJV*

You will call upon me and come and pray to me, and I will listen to you. You will seek me and find me when you seek me with all your heart. *Jeremiah 29:12-13, NIV*

This is the confidence that we have in him, that, if we ask any thing according to his will, he heareth us: And if we know that he hear us, whatsoever we ask, we know that we have the petitions that we desired of him. *1 John 5:14-15, KJV*

The effectual fervent prayer of a righteous man availeth much. *James 5:16, KJV*

Ask, and it shall be given you; seek, and ye shall find; knock, and it shall be opened unto you: For everyone that asketh receiveth; and he that seeketh findeth; and to him that knocketh it shall be opened. *Matthew 7:7-8, KJV*

It frustrates me to see bad things happen to good people. How can I be sure that God is fair?

"I am the LORD, who exercises kindness, justice and righteousness on earth, for in these I delight." *Jeremiah 9:24, NIV*

God shall bring every work into judgment, with every secret thing, whether it be good, or whether it be evil. *Ecclesiastes 12:14, KJV*

The LORD is just in all his ways, and kind in all his doings. The LORD is near to all who call upon him, to all who call upon him in truth. *Psalm 145:17-18, RSV*

The mountains shall depart, and the hills be removed; but my kindness shall not depart from thee, neither shall the covenant of my peace be removed, saith the LORD that hath mercy on thee. *Isaiah 54:10, KJV*

Who I Am to God

Sometimes I don't feel good about myself. Am I of value to God?

God created man in his own image, in the image of God created he him; male and female created he them. *Genesis 1:27, KJV*

Now you are no longer strangers to God and foreigners to heaven, but you are members of God's very own family, citizens of God's country, and you belong in God's household with every other Christian. *Ephesians 2:19, TLB*

You are precious to me and honored, and I love you. *Isaiah 43:4, TLB*

Behold, what manner of love the Father hath bestowed upon us, that we should be called the sons of God. *1 John 3:1, KJV*

Yea, I have loved thee with an everlasting love: therefore with loving-
kindness have I drawn thee. *Jeremiah
31:3, KJV*

How can I show God my love and respect?

What doth the LORD require of thee,
but to fear the LORD thy God, to walk
in all his ways, and to love him, and to
serve the LORD thy God with all thy
heart and with all thy soul.
Deuteronomy 10:12, KJV

If you love me, keep my commandments. *John 14:15, NKJV*

So then, my brothers, because of
God's great mercy to us, I make this
appeal to you: Offer yourselves as a
living sacrifice and pleasing to him.
This is the true worship that you
should offer. *Romans 12:1, TEV*

If anyone loves me, he will obey my teaching. My Father will love him, and we will come to him and make our home with him. *John 14:23, NIV*

He hath shewed thee, O man, what is good; and what doth the LORD require of thee, but to do justly, and to love mercy, and to walk humbly with thy God? *Micah 6:8, KJV*

Sometimes I feel self-conscious because age has changed my appearance. How does God see me?

You shall also be a crown of glory in the hand of the LORD, and a royal diadem in the hand of your God. *Isaiah 62:3, NKJV*

The LORD seeth not as man seeth; for man looketh on the outward appearance, but the LORD looketh on the heart. *1 Samuel 16:7, KJV*

White hair is a crown of glory and is seen most among the godly. *Proverbs 16:31, TLB*

I can't do all the things I did when I was young. What can I do for God now?

O worship the LORD in the beauty of holiness. *Psalm 96:9, KJV*

If any one is in Christ, he is a new creation; the old has passed away, behold the new has come. *2 Corinthians 5:17, RSV*

We are his workmanship, created in Christ Jesus unto god works, which God hath before ordained that we should walk in them. *Ephesians 2:10, KJV*

The righteous . . . are planted in the house of the LORD, they flourish in the courts of our God. They still bring forth fruit in old age, they are ever full of sap and green. *Psalm 92:12-14, RSV*

I'm afraid that if someday I can no longer control my actions and speech, I might dishonor the Lord.

Even to your old age and gray hairs I am he, I am he who will sustain you. I have made you and I will carry you; I will sustain you and I will rescue you. *Isaiah 46:4, NIV*

The very God of peace sanctify you wholly: and I pray God your whole spirit and soul and body be preserved blameless unto the coming of our Lord Jesus Christ. Faithful is he that calleth you, who also will do it. *1 Thessalonians 5:23-24, KJV*

The LORD, He is the one who goes before you. He will be with you, He will not leave you nor forsake you; do not fear nor be dismayed. *Deuter-onomy 31:8, NKJV*

Now unto him that is able to keep you from falling, and to present you fault-less before the presence of his glory with exceeding joy, to the only wise God our Savior, be glory and majesty, dominion and power, both now and ever. Amen. *Jude 1:24-25, KJV*

They will be like a well-watered gar-den, and they will sorrow no more . . . I will turn their mourning into glad-ness; I will give them comfort and joy instead of sorrow. *Jeremiah 31:12-13, NIV*

When I'm feeling forgotten or unimportant, how can I feel en-couraged that God hasn't forgot-ten me?

What is man, that thou are mindful of him? or the son of man, that thou visitest him? Thou madest him a little lower than the angels; thou crownedst him with glory and honour, and didst set him over the works of thy hands. *Hebrews 2:6-7, KJV*

Are not two sparrows sold for a farthing? And one of them shall not fall on the ground without your Father. But the very hairs of your head are numbered. *Matthew 10:29-30, KJV*

How precious it is, LORD, to realize that you are thinking about me constantly! I can't even count how many times a day your thoughts turn toward me. And when I waken in the morning, you are still thinking of me! *Psalm 139:17-18, TLB*

. . . neither height nor depth, nor anything else in all creation, will be able to separate us from the love of God that is in Christ Jesus our Lord. *Romans 8:39, NIV*

Children and Grandchildren

My family has been important to me all my life. Does God value my children and grandchildren?

Children's children are the crown of old men; and the glory of children are their fathers. *Proverbs 17:6, KJV*

Lo, children are an heritage of the LORD: and the fruit of the womb is his reward. As arrows are in the hand of a mighty man; so are children of the youth. Happy is the man that hath his quiver full of them. *Psalm 127:3-5a, KJV*

May the LORD bless you from Zion all the days of your life; may you see the prosperity of Jerusalem, and may you live to see your children's children. Peace be upon Israel. *Psalm 128:5-6, NIV*

May the LORD make you increase,
both you and your children. May you
be blessed by the LORD, the Maker of
heaven and earth. *Psalm 115:14, NIV*

How can my actions build a godly heritage for my children and their children?

The just man walketh in his integrity:
his children are blessed after him.
Proverbs 20:7, KJV

The counsel of the LORD standeth for
ever, the thoughts of his heart to all
generations. *Psalm 33:11, KJV*

Give yourself to the LORD; trust in
him, and he will help you; he will
make your righteousness shine like the
noonday sun. *Psalm 37:5-6, TEV*

He who fears the LORD has a secure
fortress, and for his children it will be
a refuge. *Proverbs 14:26, NIV*

And all thy children shall be taught of the LORD; and great shall be the peace of thy children. *Isaiah 54:13, KJV*

I worry about my children and my grandchildren. What can I do now to keep them growing in the Lord even after I'm not with them anymore?

Only be careful, and watch yourselves closely so that you do not forget the things your eyes have seen or let them slip from your heart as long as you live. Teach them to your children and to their children after them. *Deuteronomy 4:9, NIV*

And these words, which I command thee this day, shall be in thy heart: And thou shalt teach them diligently unto thy children, and shalt talk of them when thou sittest in thine house, and when thou walkest by the way, and when thou liest down, and when thou risest up. *Deuteronomy 6:6-7, KJV*

Gather the people together, men, and women, and children, and thy stranger that is within thy gates, that they may hear, and that they may learn, and fear the LORD your God, and observe to do all the words of this law: And that their children, which have not known any thing, may hear, and learn to fear the LORD your God. *Deuteronomy 31:12-13, KJV*

But the mercy of the LORD is from everlasting to everlasting upon them that fear him, and his righteousness unto children's children, to such as keep his covenant, and to those that remember his commandments to do them. *Psalm 103:17, KJV*

Give ear, O my people, to my law: incline your ears to the words of my mouth . . . Which we have heard and known, and our fathers have told us.

We will not hide them from their children, shewing to the generation to come the praises of the LORD, and his strength, and his wonderful works that he hath done. *Psalm 78:1, 3-4, KJV*

For he established a testimony in Jacob, and appointed a law in Israel, which he commanded our fathers, that they should make them known to their children: That the generation to come might know them . . . That they might set their hope in God, and not forget the works of God, but keep his commandments. *Psalm 78:5-6a, 7, KJV*

Sometimes I feel sad that I won't be able to look after my children and grandchildren for many more years. How can I feel assured that God will take care of them?

I have been young, and now I am old; yet I have not seen the righteous for-

saken or his children begging bread.
Psalm 37:25, RSV

The young lions do not lack, and suffer
hunger: but they that seek the LORD
shall not want any good thing. *Psalm
34:10, KJV*

He who did not grudge his own Son
but gave him up for us all—can we not
trust such a God to give us, with him,
everything else that we can need?
Romans 8:32, PHILLIPS

The righteous man leads a blameless
life; blessed are his children after him.
Proverbs 20:7, NIV

Know therefore that the LORD your
God is God; he is the faithful God,
keeping his covenant of love to a
thousand generations of those who
love him and keep his commands.
Deuteronomy 7:9, NIV

At times I'm concerned about the tensions in some of my family relationships. How does God want me to respond?

If you are offering your gift at the altar and there remember that your brother has something against you, leave your gift there in front of the altar. First go and be reconciled to your brother; then come and offer your gift. *Matthew 5:23-24, NIV*

Be kind and compassionate to one another, forgiving each other, just as in Christ God forgave you. *Ephesians 4:32, NIV*

Bear with each other and forgive whatever grievances you may have against one another. Forgive as the Lord forgave you. *Colossians 3:13, NIV*

. . . then make my joy complete by being like-minded, having the same love, being one in spirit and purpose . . . Your attitude should be the same as that of Christ Jesus. *Philippians 2:2, 5, NIV*

Try to stay out of all quarrels and seek to live a clean and holy life, for one who is not holy will not see the Lord. *Hebrews 12:14, TLB*

He who covers over an offense promotes love, but whoever repeats the matter separates close friends. *Proverbs 17:9, NIV*

Although I have brought up my children to lead godly lives, some of them are not living for God. How can I keep hoping for them?

He is patient with you, not wanting anyone to perish, but everyone to come to repentance. *2 Peter 3:9, NIV*

Have no anxiety about anything, but in everything by prayer and supplication with thanksgiving let your requests be made known to God. And the peace of God, which passes all understanding, will keep your hearts and your minds in Christ Jesus. *Philippians 4:6-7, RSV*

It is of the LORD's mercies that we are not consumed, because his compassions fail not. They are new every morning: great is thy faithfulness. It is good that a man should both hope and quietly wait for the salvation of the LORD. *Lamentations 3:22-23, 26, KJV*

Some of the choices I made as a parent were damaging to my children. I know God has forgiven me, but can God turn my mistakes into something good for my children and their children?

Glory be to God who by his mighty power at work within us is able to do far more than we would ever dare to ask or even dream of—infinitely beyond our heights prayers, desires, thoughts, or hopes. *Ephesians 3:20, TLB*

With men this is impossible; but with God all things are possible. *Matthew 19:26b, KJV*

But from everlasting to everlasting the LORD's love is with those who fear him, and his righteousness with their children's children—with those who keep his covenant and remember to obey his precepts. *Psalm 103:17-18, NIV*

If ye turn again unto the LORD, your brethren and your children shall find compassion before them that lead them captive, so that they shall come again into this land: for the LORD your God is gracious and merciful, and will not turn away his face from you, if ye return unto him. *2 Chronicles 30:9,* KJV

The LORD is nigh unto all them that call upon him, to all that call upon him in truth. He will fulfill the desire of them that fear him: he also will hear their cry, and will save them. *Psalm 145:18-19,* KJV

Although my children have families of their own, I want our extended family to grow together. How can we be unified?

Instead, speaking the truth in love, we will in all things grow up into him who is the Head, that is, Christ. *Ephesians 4:15, NIV*

And let us consider how to stimulate one another to love and good deeds, not forsaking our own assembling together, as is the habit of some but encouraging one another; and all the more, as you see the day drawing near. *Hebrews 10:24-25, NASB*

Therefore encourage one another, and build up one another, just as you also are doing. *1 Thessalonians 5:11, NASB*

Speak to one another with psalms, hymns and spiritual songs. Sing and make music in your heart to the Lord, always giving thanks to God the Father for everything in the name of our Lord Jesus Christ. *Ephesians 5:19-20, NIV*

You should be like one big happy family, full of sympathy toward each other, loving one another with tender

hearts and humble minds. *1 Peter 3:8,*
TLB

Share each other's troubles and problems, and so obey our Lord's command. *Galatians 6:2, TLB*

When I'm Hurting Physically

I feel alone with my physical pain; no one else can feel it with me. How can I know God is with me when I'm hurting?

He hath said, "I will never leave thee, nor forsake thee." *Hebrews 13:5, KJV*

Lo, I am with you alway, even unto the end of the world. *Matthew 28:20, KJV*

Then shalt thou call, and the LORD shall answer; thou shalt cry, and he shall say, Here I am. *Isaiah 58:9, KJV*

How precious it is, Lord, to realize that you are thinking about me constantly! I can't even count how many times a day your thoughts turn toward me. And when I waken in the morning, you are still thinking of me! *Psalm 139:17-18, TLB*

I will be your God through all your lifetime, yes, even when your hair is white with age. I made you and I will care for you. I will carry you along and be your Savior. *Isaiah 46:4, TLB*

You hear, O LORD, the desire of the afflicted; you encouraged them, and you listen to their cry, defending the fatherless and the oppressed, in order that man, who is of the earth, may terrify no more. *Psalm 10:17-18, NIV*

If I become inarticulate or confused, will I still be able to communicate with God?

The Spirit helps us in our weakness. We do not know what we ought to pray, but the Spirit himself intercedes for us with groans that words cannot express. *Romans 8:26, NIV*

O LORD, you have searched me and you know me. You know when I sit and when I rise; you perceive my thoughts from afar. You discern my going out and my lying down; you are familiar with all my ways. Before a word is on my tongue you know it completely, O LORD. *Psalm 139:1-4, NIV*

He withdraweth not his eyes from the righteous. *Job 36:7a, KJV*

When I see those dear to me suffering, I sometimes doubt God's goodness. How can I be reminded that he is a caring God?

He has not despised or disdained the suffering of the afflicted one; he has not hidden his face from him but has listened to his cry for help. *Psalm 22:24, NIV*

The mountains may depart and the hills be removed, but my steadfast love shall not depart from you, and my covenant of peace shall not be removed, says the LORD, who has compassion on you. *Isaiah 54:10, RSV*

The LORD longs to be gracious to you; he rises to show you compassion. For the LORD is a God of justice. Blessed are all who wait for him! *Isaiah 30:18, NIV*

Blessed be the God and Father of our Lord Jesus Christ, the Father of mercies and God of all comfort, who comforts us in all our affliction, so that we may be able to comfort those who are in any affliction, with the comfort with which we ourselves are comforted by God. For as we share abundantly in Christ's sufferings, so through Christ we share abundantly in comfort too. *2 Corinthians 1:3-5, RSV*

We know that all things work together for good to them that love God, to them who are called according to his purpose. *Romans 8:28, KJV*

Sometimes my ongoing physical discomfort makes me depressed or discouraged. How can I tap into the Source of joy when I feel down?

Base your happiness on your hope in Christ. When trials come, endure them patiently; steadfastly maintain the habit of prayer. *Romans 12:12, PHILLIPS*

The LORD is close to the brokenhearted and saves those who are crushed in spirit. *Psalm 34:18, NIV*

O my soul, why be so gloomy and discouraged? Trust in God! I shall again praise him for his wondrous help; he will make me smile again, for he is my God! *Psalm 43:5, TLB*

Our light affliction, which is but for a moment, worketh for us a far more exceeding and eternal weight of glory; while we look not at the things which are seen, but at the things which are not seen: for the things which are seen are temporal; but the things which are not seen are eternal. *2 Corinthians 4:17-18, KJV*

Will God give me the strength to endure my sickness and pain?

The LORD is my light and my salvation; whom shall I fear? The LORD is the strength of my life; of whom shall I be afraid? *Psalm 27:1, KJV*

Cast your cares on the LORD and he will sustain you; he will never let the righteous fall. *Psalm 55:22, NIV*

My God shall supply all your need according to his riches in glory by Christ Jesus. *Philippians 4:19, KJV*

Trust in the Lord God always, for in the Lord Jehovah is your everlasting strength. *Isaiah 26:4, TLB*

He giveth power to the faint and to them that have no might he increaseth strength. Even the youths shall faint and be weary, and the young men shall utterly fall: but they that wait upon the LORD shall renew their strength; they shall mount up with wings as eagles; they shall run and not be weary; and they shall walk, and not faint. *Isaiah 40:29-31, KJV*

Sometimes when I'm afraid or anxious, I feel physically ill. How can I feel secure and unafraid?

When thou passest through the waters, I will be with thee; and through the rivers, they shall not overflow thee: when thou walkest through the fire, thou shalt not be burned; neither shall the flame kindle upon thee. For I am the LORD thy God, the Holy One of Israel, thy Saviour. *Isaiah 43:2-3, KJV*

Just as you trusted Christ to save you, trust him, too, for each day's problems; live in vital union with him. *Colossians 2:6, TLB*

Let him have all your worries and cares, for he is always thinking about you and watching everything that concerns you. *1 Peter 5:7, TLB*

Fear not: for I have redeemed thee, I have called thee by thy name; thou are mine. *Isaiah 43:1, KJV*

When physical limitations prevent me from leaving the house, I stay at home and pray. How can I know my prayers will accomplish anything?

Whatsoever we ask, we receive of him, because we keep his commandments, and do those things that are pleasing in his sight. *1 John 3:22, KJV*

I will pray morning, noon, and night, pleading aloud with God; and he will hear and answer. *Psalm 55:17, TLB*

Have no anxiety about anything, but in everything, by prayer and supplication with thanksgiving let your requests be made known to God. And the peace of God, which passes all understanding, will keep your hearts and minds in Christ Jesus. *Philippians 4:6-7, RSV*

Even before they finish praying to me, I will answer their prayers. *Isaiah 65:24,* TEV

This is the confidence which we have in him, that if we ask anything according to his will he hears us. *1 John 5:14,* RSV

Can the Lord help me rest at night when I am unable to sleep?

I lie down and sleep; I wake again, for the LORD sustains me. *Psalm 3:5,* RSV

He giveth his beloved sleep. *Psalm 127:2b,* KJV

Come to me, all you who are weary and burdened, and I will give you rest. Take my yoke upon you and learn from me, for I am gentle and humble in heart, and you will find rest for your souls. For my yoke is easy and my burden is light. *Matthew 11:28-30,* NIV

He who dwells in the shelter of the Most High will rest in the shadow of the Almighty. *Psalm 91:1, NIV*

On days when I feel physically weak, how can I help my faith grow strong?

We do not lose heart. Though outwardly we are wasting away, yet inwardly we are being renewed day by day. For our light and momentary troubles are achieving for us an eternal weight of glory that far outweighs them all. So we fix our eyes not on what is seen, but on what is unseen. For what is seen is temporary, but what is unseen is eternal. *2 Corinthians 4:16-18, NIV*

Let us therefore come boldly unto the throne of grace, that we may obtain mercy, and find grace to help in time of need. *Hebrews 4:16, KJV*

Even when we are too weak to have any faith left, he remains faithful to us and will help us, for he cannot disown us who are part of himself, and he will always carry out his promises to us. *2 Timothy 2:13, TLB*

Sometimes I'm afraid that my physical limitations will be embarrassing to my loved ones.

Fear not; for thou shalt not be ashamed: neither be thou confounded; for thou shalt not be put to shame . . . With everlasting kindness will I have mercy on thee, saith the LORD thy Redeemer. *Isaiah 54:4a, 8b, KJV*

I will lift up mine eyes unto the hills, from whence cometh my help. My help cometh from the LORD, which made heaven and earth. He will not suffer thy foot to be moved: he that keepeth thee will not slumber. The

LORD is thy shade upon thy right hand.
Psalm 121:1-3, 5, KJV

I the LORD thy God will hold thy right
hand, saying unto thee, Fear not; I will
help thee. *Isaiah 41:13, KJV*

I will bring the blind by a way that they
knew not; I will lead them in paths that
they have not known: I will make
darkness light before them, and
crooked things straight. These things
will I do unto them, and not forsake
them. *Isaiah 42:16, KJV*

When Circumstances Around Me Are Hard

As my life changes, I sometimes feel confused and unstable. Can God provide the guidance and safety I need?

The LORD, he it is that doth go before thee; he will be with thee, he will not fail thee, neither forsake thee: fear not, neither be dismayed. *Deuteronomy 31:8, KJV*

Know therefore that the LORD your God, He is God, the faithful God, who keeps His covenant and His loving-kindness to a thousandth generation with those who love Him and keep His commandments. *Deuteronomy 7:9, NASB*

God hath not given us the spirit of fear; but of power, and of love, and of a sound mind. *2 Timothy 1:7, KJV*

He will never let me stumble, slip or fall. For he is always watching, never sleeping. Jehovah himself is caring for you! He is your defender. He protects you day and night. He keeps you from all evil, and preserves your life. He keeps his eye upon you as you come and go, and always guards you. *Psalm 121:3-8, TLB*

My grace is sufficient for thee: for my strength is made perfect in weakness. *2 Corinthians 12:9, KJV*

Let him have all your worries and cares, for he is always thinking about you and watching everything that concerns you. *1 Peter 5:7, TLB*

I feel anxious because others are making decisions for me.

The LORD shall preserve thee from all evil: he shall preserve thy soul. The LORD shall preserve thy going out and thy coming in from this time forth, and even for evermore. *Psalm 121:7-8, KJV*

The LORD is my strength and my shield; my heart trusts in him, and I am helped. My heart leaps for joy and I will give thanks to him in song. *Psalm 28:7, NIV*

Thou wilt keep him in perfect peace, whose mind is stayed on thee: because he trusteth in thee. *Isaiah 26:3, KJV*

If God be for us, who can be against us? *Romans 8:31, KJV*

Wait on the LORD: be of good courage, and he shall strengthen thine heart: wait, I say, on the LORD. *Psalm 27:14, KJV*

How can I find peace when I feel anxious about the unknown, uncertain things in life?

Have no anxiety about anything, but in everything by prayer and supplication with thanksgiving let your requests be made known to God. And the peace of God, which passes all understanding, will keep your hearts and your minds in Christ Jesus. *Philippians 4:6-7, RSV*

Peace I leave with you, my peace I give unto you; not as the world giveth, give I unto you. Let not your heart be troubled, neither let it be afraid. *John 14:27, KJV*

These things I have spoken unto you, that in me ye might have peace. In the world ye shall have tribulation: but be of good cheer; I have overcome the world. *John 16:33, KJV*

The L𝗈rd loves the just and will not forsake his faithful ones. They will be protected forever. *Psalm 37:28, NIV*

As old friends and family members pass away or move away from me, I am often sad. How can I feel encouraged by God?

Most assuredly, I say to you that you will weep and lament, but the world will rejoice; and you will be sorrowful, but your sorrow shall be turned into joy. *John 16:20, NKJV*

He healeth the broken in heart, and bindeth up their wounds. *Psalm 147:3, KJV*

The L𝗈rd your God is a merciful God; he will not abandon or destroy you or forget the covenant with your forefathers, which he confirmed to them by oath. *Deuteronomy 4:31, NIV*

Sometimes I worry about finances. Will God provide for my needs?

The Lord himself is my inheritance, my prize. He is my food and drink, my highest joy! He guards all that is mine. He sees that I am given pleasant brooks and meadows as my share! What a wonderful inheritance! *Psalm 16:5-6, TLB*

He who did not grudge his own Son but gave him up for us all—can we not trust such a God to give us, with him, everything else that we can need? *Romans 8:32, PHILLIPS*

I will always guide you and satisfy you with good things. I will keep you strong and well. You will be like a garden that has plenty of water, like a spring of water that never goes dry. *Isaiah 58:11, TEV*

You open your hand and satisfy the desire of every living thing. The LORD is righteous in all his ways and loving toward all he has made. The LORD is near to all who call on him in truth. He fulfills the desires of those who fear him; he hears their cry and saves them. *Psalm 145:16-19, NIV*

It's hard for me not to worry about money and about being a financial burden to my family. How does God want me to handle dependency?

Cast all your anxieties on him, for he cares about you. *1 Peter 5:7, RSV*

The LORD thy God hath blessed thee in all the works of they hand: he knoweth thy walking through this great wilderness . . . the LORD thy God hath been with thee; thou hast lacked nothing. *Deuteronomy 2:7, KJV*

My God shall supply all your need
according to his riches in glory by
Christ Jesus. *Philippians 4:19, KJV*

I have been young, and now I am old;
yet I have not seen the righteous for-
saken or his children begging bread.
Psalm 37:25, RSV

**Sometimes I feel resentful when I
see others enjoying comfort and
wealth. Can God help me be glad
for them and thankful for what I
have?**

Be still before the LORD, and wait
patiently for him; fret not yourself
over him who prospers in his way ...
Refrain from anger, and forsake
wrath! Fret not yourself; it tends only
to evil. *Psalm 37:7-8, RSV*

Let all bitterness, and wrath, and
anger, and clamour, and evil speaking,

be put away from you, with all malice: And be ye kind one to another, tender-hearted, forgiving one another, even as God for Christ's sake hath forgiven you. *Ephesians 4:31-32, KJV*

O my soul, don't be discouraged. Don't be upset. Expect God to act! For I know that I shall again have plenty of reason to praise him for all that he will do. He is my help! He is my God! *Psalm 42:11, TLB*

Trust in him at all times; ye people, pour out your heart before him: God is a refuge for us. *Psalm 62:8, KJV*

How can I develop a deep and lasting faith—one that doesn't shift from day to day?

The Lord will make you go through hard times, but he himself will be there to teach you, and you will not have to search for him any more. If you wander off the road to the right or the left, you will hear his voice behind you saying, "Here is the road. Follow it." *Isaiah 30:20-21, TEV*

Seek the LORD and his strength, seek his face continually. *1 Chronicles 16:11, KJV*

The Comforter, which is the Holy Ghost, whom the Father will send in my name, he shall teach you all things, and bring all things to your remembrance, whatsoever I have said unto you. *John 14:26, KJV*

When all kinds of trials and temptations crowd into your lives, my brothers, don't resent them as intruders, but welcome them as friends! Realize that they come to test your faith and to produce in you the quality of endurance. *James 1:2-3, PHILLIPS*

Death and the Hope of Heaven

When I think about death, it seems so final. How can I know that I have eternal life?

God so loved the world that he gave his only begotten Son, that whosoever believeth in him should not perish, but have everlasting life. *John 3:16, KJV*

God hath given to us eternal life, and this life is in his Son. He that hath the Son hath life; and he that hath not the Son of God hath not life. These things have I written unto you that believe on the name of the Son of God: that ye may know that ye have eternal life, and that ye may believe on the name of the Son of God. *1 John 5:11-13, KJV*

It is God himself who makes us, together with you, sure of our life in union with Christ; it is God himself who has set us apart, who has placed his mark of ownership upon us, and who has given us the Holy Spirit in our hearts as the guarantee of all that he has in store for us. *2 Corinthians 1:21-22, TEV*

Not by works of righteousness which we have done, but according to his mercy he saved us, by the washing of regeneration, and renewing of the Holy Ghost; which he shed on us abundantly through Jesus Christ our Saviour; That being justified by his grace, we should be made heirs according to the hope of eternal life. *Titus 3:5-7, KJV*

The thief comes only to steal and kill and destroy; I have come that they may have life, and have it to the full. *John 10:10, NIV*

When Christ, who is our life, shall appear, then shall ye also appear with him in glory. *Colossians 3:3, KJV*

Even though I know I'll go to be with the Lord, sometimes I am afraid of dying. Can God relieve my fears about death?

He too shared in their humanity so that by his death he might destroy him who holds the power of death—that is, the devil—and free those who all their lives were held in slavery by their fear of death. *Hebrews 2:14-15, NIV*

I sought the LORD, and he heard me, and delivered me from all my fears. *Psalm 34:4, KJV*

For as in Adam all die, even so in Christ shall all be made alive. . . . The last enemy that shall be destroyed is death. . . . But thanks be to God, which giveth us the victory through our LORD Jesus Christ. *1 Corinthians 15:22, 26, 57, KJV*

He will swallow up death in victory; and the LORD God will wipe away tears from off all the faces; and the rebuke of the people shall he take away from off all the earth: for the LORD hath spoken it. *Isaiah 25:8, KJV*

I will ransom them from the power of the grave; I will redeem them from death. Where, O death, are your plagues? Where, O grave, is your destruction? *Hosea 13:14, NIV*

When I think about dying, I feel lonely. Will God be with me when I die?

Yea, though I walk through the valley of the shadow of death, I will fear no evil: for thou art with me; thy rod and thy staff they comfort me. *Psalm 23:4, KJV*

For such is God, our God forever and ever; He will guide us until death. *Psalm 48:14, NASB*

I am persuaded, that neither death, nor life, nor angels, nor principalities, nor powers, nor things present, nor things to come, nor height, nor depth, nor any other creature, shall be able to separate us from the love of God, which is in Christ Jesus our LORD. *Romans 8:38-39, KJV*

He will never abandon his people. They will be kept safe forever. *Psalm 37:28, TLB*

God will redeem my soul from the power of the grave: for he shall receive me. *Psalm 49:15, KJV*

I am continually with thee: thou hast holden me by my right hand. Thou shalt guide me with thy counsel, and afterward receive me to glory. *Psalm 73:23-24, KJV*

I'm looking forward to heaven. What will it be like?

In my Father's house are many mansions: if it were not so, I would have told you. I go to prepare a place for you. *John 14:2, KJV*

The city has no need of sun or moon to shine upon it, for the glory of God is its light, and its lamp is the Lamb. *Revelation 21:23, RSV*

To him that overcometh will I give to eat of the tree of life, which is in the midst of the paradise of God. *Revelation 2:7, KJV*

Now there is in store for me the crown of righteousness, which the Lord, the righteous Judge, will award to me on that day—not only to me, but also to all who have longed for his appearing. *2 Timothy 4:8, NIV*

I saw a new heaven and a new earth ... And I heard a great voice out of heaven saying, Behold, the tabernacle of God is with men, and he will dwell with them, and they shall be his people, and God himself shall be with them, and be their God. *Revelation 21:1, 3, KJV*

God shall wipe away all tears from their eyes; and there shall be no more death, neither sorrow, nor crying, neither shall there be any more pain: for the former things are passed away ... Behold I make all things new. *Revelation 21:4-5, KJV*

Many of my dearest friends and family members have died. Where can I find comfort?

For if we believe that Jesus died and rose again, even so them also which sleep in Jesus will God bring with him.

For this we say unto you by the word of the Lord, that we which are alive and remain unto the coming of the Lord shall not prevent them which are asleep. *1 Thessalonians 4:14-15, KJV*

I, even I, am he that comforteth you. *Isaiah 51:12, KJV*

He healeth the broken in heart, and bindeth up their wounds. *Psalm 147:3, KJV*

Blessed be God, even the Father of our Lord Jesus Christ, the Father of mercies, and the God of all comfort; who comforted us in all our tribulation, that we may be able to comfort them which are in any trouble, by the comfort wherewith we ourselves are comforted of God. *2 Corinthians 1:3-4, KJV*

The Abundant Life

Most of my life is behind me now. Does God want me to make certain plans for the years ahead?

One thing I do, forgetting what lies behind and straining forward to what lies ahead, I press on toward the goal for the prize of the upward call of God in Christ Jesus. *Philippians 3:13-14, RSV*

Do your best to present yourself to God as one approved, a workman who does not need to be ashamed and who correctly handles the word of truth. *2 Timothy 2:15, NIV*

He guides the humble in what is right and teaches them his way. *Psalm 25:9, NIV*

As you have therefore received Christ Jesus the Lord, so walk in him: rooted and built up in him, and established in the faith, as you have been taught, abounding in it with thanksgiving. *Colossians 2:6-7, NKJV*

We can be mirrors that brightly reflect the glory of the Lord. And as the Spirit of the Lord works within us, we become more and more like him. *2 Corinthians 3:18, TLB*

You did not choose Me, but I chose you, and appointed you, that you should go and bear fruit, and that your fruit should remain: that whatever you ask the Father in My name, He may give you. *John 15:16, NKJV*

You chart the path ahead of me, and tell me where to stop and rest. Every moment, you know where I am. You both precede and follow me, and place your hand of blessing on my head. *Psalm 139:3, 5, TLB*

I have received so much from God. What can I do for him?

Thou shalt love the Lord thy God with all thy heart, and with all thy soul, and with all thy mind. This is the first and great commandment. *Matthew 22:37-38, KJV*

If ye love me, keep my commandments. *John 14:15, KJV*

This is how we know what love is: Jesus Christ laid down his life for us. And we ought to lay down our lives for our brothers. *1 John 3:16, NIV*

Whatever you do, work at it with all your heart, as working for the Lord, not for men, since you know that you will receive an inheritance from the Lord as a reward. It is the Lord Christ you are serving. *Colossians 3:23-24, NIV*

Every day I will praise you and extol your name for ever and ever. *Psalm 145:2, NIV*

I haven't read the Bible much during my life. I have more time now. Will God really speak to me?

Your words are what sustain me; they are food to my hungry soul. They bring joy to my sorrowing heart and delight me. *Jeremiah 15:16, TLB*

If ye continue in my word, then ye are my disciples indeed; and ye shall know the truth, and the truth shall make you free. *John 8:31-32, KJV*

The word of God is living and active. Sharper than any double-edged sword, it penetrates even to dividing soul and spirit, joints and marrow; it judges the thoughts and attitudes of the heart. *Hebrews 4:12, NIV*

All those words which were written long ago are meant to each us today; so that we may be encouraged to endure and to go on hoping in our own time. *Romans 15:4, PHILLIPS*

All Scripture is given by inspiration of God, and is profitable for doctrine, for reproof, for correction, for instruction in righteousness: That the man of God may be perfect, thoroughly furnished unto all good works. *2 Timothy 3:16-17, KJV*

Thy word is a lamp unto my feet, and a light unto my path. The entrance of thy words giveth light; it giveth understanding unto the simple. *Psalm 119:105, 130, KJV*

For many, old age is a time of sadness and discomfort. How can I be full of joy?

I will rejoice in the LORD, I will joy in the God of my salvation. *Habakkuk 3:18, KJV*

Thou dost show me the path of life; in thy presence there is fulness of joy, in thy right hand are pleasures for evermore. *Psalm 16:11, RSV*

Delight yourselves in the Lord, yes, find your joy in him at all times . . . Never forget the nearness of your Lord. *Philippians 4:4-5, PHILLIPS*

I will greatly rejoice in the LORD, my soul shall be joyful in my God; for he hath clothed me with the garments of salvation, he hath covered me with the robe of righteousness, as a bridegroom decketh himself with ornaments, and as a bride adorneth herself with her jewels. *Isaiah 61:10, KJV*

Just as you received Christ Jesus the Lord, so go on living in him—in simple faith. Yes, be rooted in him and founded upon him, continually strengthened by the faith as you were taught it and your lives will overflow with joy and thankfulness. *Colossians 2:6-7, PHILLIPS*

I seem to be spending more and more time alone. How can I turn this into something good rather than letting it get me down?

Singing and making melody in your heart to the Lord; Giving thanks always for all things unto God and the Father in the name of our Lord Jesus Christ. *Ephesians 5:19b-20, KJV*

Base your happiness on your hope in Christ. When trials come endure them patiently; steadfastly maintain the habit of prayer. *Romans 12:12, PHILLIPS*

Let each of you look not only to his own interests, but also to the interests of others. *Philippians 2:4, RSV*

I will remember the works of the Lord: surely I will remember thy wonders of old. I will meditate also of all thy work, and talk of thy doings. *Psalm 77:11-12, KJV*

As I am becoming more limited in my ability to get out or to travel, how can I keep sharing my faith and my Christian experience with others?

The righteous will flourish like a palm tree, they will grow like a cedar of Lebanon; planted in the house of the LORD, they will flourish in the courts of our God. They will still bear fruit in old age, they will stay fresh and green, proclaiming, "The LORD is upright; he is my Rock, and there is no wickedness in him." *Psalm 92:12-15, NIV*

Sanctify the Lord God in your hearts: and be ready always to give an answer to every man that asketh you a reason of the hope that is in you with meekness and fear. *1 Peter 3:15, KJV*

You may live a life worthy of the Lord and may please him in every way: bearing fruit in every good work, growing in the knowledge of God, being strengthened with all power according to his glorious might so that you may have great endurance and patience, and joyfully giving thanks to the Father, who has qualified you to share in the inheritance of the saints in the kingdom of light. *Colossians 1:10-12, NIV*

For God did not give us a spirit of timidity, but a spirit of power, of love

and of self-discipline. *2 Timothy 1:7,*
NIV

*Because of physical limitations, I
am unable to serve the Lord in the
way I used to. How can I serve him
now?*

Giving all diligence, add to your faith
virtue; and to virtue knowledge; and to
knowledge temperance; and to
temperance patience; and to patience
godliness; and to godliness brotherly
kindness; and to brotherly kindness
charity. For if these things be in you,
and abound, they make you that ye
shall neither be barren nor unfruitful
in the knowledge of our Lord Jesus
Christ. *2 Peter 1:5-8, KJV*

Warn them that are unruly, comfort the
feebleminded, support the weak, be
patient toward all men. See that none
render evil for evil unto any man; but

ever follow that which is good, both among yourselves, and to all men. Rejoice evermore. Pray without ceasing. In every thing give thanks: for this is the will of God in Christ Jesus concerning you. *1 Thessalonians 5:14-18, KJV*

O worship the Lord in the beauty of holiness. *Psalm 96:9, KJV*

Then the King will say to those on his right hand, Come, you blessed of my Father, inherit the kingdom prepared for you from the foundation of the world: for I was hungry, and you gave me food: I was thirsty, and you gave me drink: I was a stranger, and you took me in: I was naked, and you clothed me: I was sick, and you visited me: I was in prison, and you came to me. Inasmuch as you did it unto one of the least of these my brethren, you did it to me. *Matthew 25:34-36, 40, NKJV*

Now that I am older, I still want to get excited about and be involved in life, but what do I have to look forward to?

I am come that they might have life, and that they might have it more abundantly. *John 10:10b, KJV*

I know the plans I have for you, says the Lord, plans for welfare and not for evil, to give you a future and a hope. *Jeremiah 29:11, RSV*

The Spirit Himself bears witness with our spirit that we are children of God, and if children, heirs also, heirs of God and fellow heirs with Christ, if indeed we suffer with Him in order that we may also be glorified with Him. *Romans 8:16-17, NASB*

Thou dost show me the path of life; in thy presence there is fulness of joy, in thy right hand are pleasures forevermore. *Psalm 16:11, RSV*

You have everything when you have Christ, and you are filled with God through your union with Christ. *Colossians 2:10, TLB*

He guides the humble in what is right and teaches them his way. Who, then, is the man that fears the LORD? He will instruct him in the way chosen for him. *Psalm 25:9, 12, NIV*

Prayer Page

DATE	PRAYER		

DATE	PRAYER		

DATE   **PRAYER**

_____

_____

_____

_____

_____

DATE   **PRAYER**

_____

_____

_____

_____

_____

DATE   PRAYER
_____
_____
_____
_____
_____
_____
_____

DATE   PRAYER
_____
_____
_____
_____
_____
_____

DATE	PRAYER

DATE	PRAYER

Continue this prayer journal in your own
notebook.

More Books for Christian Living

BIBLE INDEX POCKETBOOK. This easy-to-read index contains references to more than 1000 important subjects. Useful with any translation.

THE BIBLE TELLS ME SO: God's Promises for Kids. The Bible's answers to questions kids ask most.

PARENT'S PROMISE POCKETBOOK. Hundreds of verses highlight the blessings and challenges of parenting.

PERSONAL PROMISE POCKETBOOK. Discover how God's promises and purposes correspond to many of your needs. The Four-Step System will help you claim and retain these verses.

POCKET GUIDE TO THE NEW TESTAMENT. Handy outlines and summaries of content and theological themes for each book of the New Testament.

POCKET GUIDE TO THE OLD TESTAMENT. Handy outlines and summaries of content and theological themes for each book of the Old Testament.

STUDENT PROMISE POCKETBOOK. Special answers from God's Word for students and young adults, featuring the Four-Step System that helps you personalize and claim God's promises.

Order from your favorite bookstore or write:

...old Shaw Publishers, Box 567, Wheaton, IL